Divya Victor's *Natural Subjects*, a tough-mi & subtly open-ended poem, closes in on the locating the small but bureaucratically nebu photo and opening up the multi-layered points or stress and dislocated violence that frame marks. But that only gets at a little bit of what *Natural Subjects* does. I register things like an offhand cubist tonality, a witty examination of scale, a spin of the frame to let character-versions of Eliza Doolittle, Hedda Gabbler, and fraülein Maria in, and the shaping of poetic material that comes from many sources without leaning on them. Nothing is telegraphed. The book keeps opening each time I pass through.

Anselm Berrigan, author of *Notes from Irrelevance*

"May I see your passport, please?" What are you a citizen of? What subject to? Are you natural or naturalized? What have you sworn to and will you tell true? Divya Victor, true to form in wit and poetic acuteness, has made a book about nations, nationality, and their notions by showing documents, facts, fictional and real heroines, instructions for assembly, and lyric lists that makes readers acknowledge their own disassembly, distribution, and/ or dispersal in an on-going diaspora. This acute work by Victor teases civic ideologies in all their motley, pervasive constructions by writing from multiple subjectivities and engineering defiance, struggles with agency, language play, appropriated commentaries, and revelations of loss. A multi-faceted book of high interest.

Rachel Blau DuPlessis, author of *Drafts*

A mandala of homeland motifs and constellations that are numbered but not named bursts, at the start of Divya Victor's strangely painful and real new book, to reveal: talons, attempts, a "pose." These initiating frames take us through a naturalization process – from the gathering of biometric data to the duplex-pomegranate-linoleum reverie of the pledge ceremony itself. Questions of "exit" and "enunciation" accrue a "blunt hum" as the book progresses. Lit from within by an "opal glass shade" or the "violent and excited" intake. Yet never clarified. Here, for example, is Dimple Kapadia, taking the stage like late onset "logopoeia." Are you a "great scholar"? Are you a "lover"? Did you make your home in the trampled lot behind the Edison IKEA? Did you "maybe write things"? Victor has written a book that is both heart-breaking and a brilliant, effervescent and dark joke.

Bhanu Kapil, author of *Schizophrene*

NATURAL SUBJECTS

Natural Subjects by Divya Victor
Published by Trembling Pillow Press
New Orleans, LA
ISBN-13: 978-0-9887257-7-5
Copyright © 2014 by Divya Victor

All Rights Reserved. No part of this book may be reproduced in any form without permission from the publisher with the exception of brief passages cited or for educational purposes. Reproduction for commercial use is prohibited except by permission of the author.

Typesetting and Design: Megan Burns
Author Photo: Selfie
Cover Art: and Design: Nicolas Mugavero

Trembling
Pillow
PRESS

NATURAL SUBJECTS
BY DIVYA VICTOR

Bob Kaufman (1925-1986)
detail of woodcut by Kristin Wetterhahn

WINNER OF THE 2014 BOB KAUFMAN BOOK PRIZE
SELECTED BY ANSELM BERRIGAN

NATURAL SUBJECTS

Divya Victor

For my mother, father, and grandmother — my migrant centers.

I   NATURAL SUBJECTS

II   PASSPORT PHOTO OF ELIZA DOOLITTLE

III   PASSPORT PHOTO SELFIE

IV   PASSPORT PHOTO OF FRÄULEIN MARIA

V   PASSPORT PHOTO OF HEDDA GABLER

VI   PASSPORT PHOTOS OF MAD & MADDENING CHILDS

VII   THIS NATURAL SUBJECT REQUIRES ASSEMBLY

Tell me I'm your National Anthem

Ooh, yeah, baby, bow down

Making me so wild now

Tell me I'm your National Anthem

Sugar, sugar, how now

Take your body down town

Red, white, blue is in the sky

Summer's in the air and

Baby, heaven's in your eyes

I'm your National Anthem

Money is the anthem

God, you're so handsome

Money is the anthem

Of success

— Lana Del Rey, *National Anthem*

"I never knew how a bunch of people half a world away chose a random town in New Jersey to populate. Were they from some Indian state that got made fun of by all the other Indian states and didn't want to give up that feeling? Are the malls in India that bad? Did we accidentally keep numbering our parkway exits all the way to Mumbai?

[...]

Eventually, there were enough Indians in Edison to change the culture. At which point my townsfolk started calling the new Edisonians "dot heads." One kid I knew in high school drove down an Indian-dense street yelling for its residents to "go home to India." In retrospect, I question just how good our schools were if "dot heads" was the best racist insult we could come up with for a group of people whose gods have multiple arms and an elephant nose."

—Joel Stein, "My Own Private India: How the Jersey town named for Thomas Edison Became Home to the all-American Guindian," *TIME*, July 2010

During the years that this book was being written, The United States Immigration and Naturalization Service (INS) was an autonomous agency in the U.S. Department of Justice. Today, it has been folded into the cluster of human services known as the Department of Homeland Security.

A white American
eagle appears
in a circular blue field

The eagle's wings
break through an inner
red ring into an outer
white ring

The eagle's talon
on the left holds
an olive branch
with 13 leaves
& 13 seeds

The eagle's talon
on the right grasps
13 arrows
pointed outward

The eagle's breast
hosts a shield carved
into three sections
that represent the American homeland
—air, land, and sea.

a dark blue sky containing 22 stars

white mountains behind a green plain underneath a light blue sky

four waves of the oceans alternating light and dark blue separated by white
lines

all mine

all mine

by the dawn's early light
through the perilous fight
O'er the ramparts we watched
through the mists of the deep
O'er the towering steep
from the terror of flight
in the gloom of the grave
O'er the land of the free
& the home of the brave

Naturalization is the process through which U.S. citizenship is conferred upon a foreign citizen or national after he or she fulfills the requirements established by Congress in the Immigration and Nationality Act.

I is a period of continuous residence and physical presence in the United States

I is a knowledge and understanding of U.S. history and government

I is an ability to read, write, and speak English

I is good moral character

I is an attachment to the principles of the U.S. Constitution

I is a favorable disposition toward the United States

I have fulfilled the general requirements for administrative naturalization

OF LIFE

LIBERTY

& THE

PURSUIT

OF *HA*

OF *HA*

OF *HA*

BREAKING NEWS: YOU WILL REQUIRE AN ABILITY TO READ,
WRITE, AND SPEAK GOOD MORAL CHARACTER;
AN ABILITY TO READ, WRITE, AND SPEAK A
FAVORABLE DISPOSITION TOWARD THE UNITED
STATES. YOU WILL READ, WRITE, AND SPEAK
AN ATTACHMENT TO THE PRINCIPLES OF THE
U.S.CONSTITUTION

I tell myself: "You will be a natural"

BREAKING NEWS: YOU ARE NOT A TRAVEL DOCUMENT AND WILL
                      NOT BE ACCEPTED AS SUCH; YOU ARE NOT A
                      HOLDER OF THE TRAVEL DOCUMENT AND WILL
                      NOT BE ACCEPTED AS SUCH; YOU ARE NOT
                      PERMITTED TO BE THE DOCUMENT OF YOUR
                      SPOUSE OR CHILDREN AND WILL NOT BE HELD
                      BY THEM AS SUCH; YOU ARE BEHOLDEN AT THE
                      PORT OF ENTRY AND WILL BE PERMITTED TO
                      PRESENT YOUR BODY TO THE OFFICER UPON
                      YOUR ARRIVAL AND WILL BE ACCEPTED AS
                      SUCH BY THE OFFICER OF THE UNITED STATES
                      OF AMERICA

You tell me: "You will need travel documents"

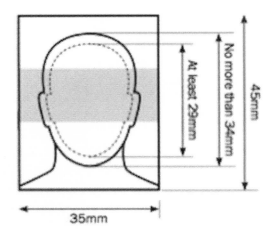

They tell me: "We encourage the subject to have a natural expression"

BREAKING NEWS: WE HAVE ACCOMPANIED NO CHILD OR SPOUSE.
                      WE HAVE OUR NAMES ENDORSED HEREIN. WE
                      HAVE PERFORMED SOME BODY'S JOURNEY.

my body lies over the ocean

my body lies over the sea

my body lies over the ocean

O bring back my body to me

Get $2.00 OFF
Passport Photos

Print this coupon and bring it to any CVS/pharmacy
store and **receive $2.00 off your passport photo
in the CVS Photo Center. Valid thru 12/31/13.**

CVS Photo

Touchscreen registers:
Scan the barcode. If unable to scan, select the "Item #"
from the "Sales" tab, then key in the 5-digit coupon code
and press "Enter".

Traditional registers:
Scan the barcode. If unable to scan, key in the 5-digit
coupon code and press "Enter".

Cashier, please scan bar code or enter
coupon code: 46772

*Maximum $2.00 value. Valid in-store only. Tax charged on pre-coupon price where required. Limit one per customer.
CVS/pharmacy will not honor any facsimile, photocopy or any other reproduction of this coupon. No cash back. Valid thru
12/31/13.

Please note: All images may not print in your internet browser. Just print the coupon in black and white or color and bring
it to the store as is.

My new home: No more than 34mm
At least 29mm

From here to there

Profile: Passing Attempt 1

profile comes from the Italian *profilare*
— *filare* to spin thread
to give face to the trace of your name
to be needled to pull a thread through
to be seen as a document of a filament
your thread-like body spun
a fiber in tow, from town to town

to be especially so a person in such and such a way
to be especially so a flattened head. to be seen in profile
is to be seen from one side. on the page
from a position in which the subject is more
than half turned away from the onlooker.

Profile: Passing Attempt 2

that the face itself is not proof of its situation
to be seen in a document
to have your face in a folder
marked in a catalogue of clues leading to
a location of another face to face
the trace of your name. to be drawn
as an outline of a dotted leap across
oceans and have your brow be a reminder
a summary of salutes. from your crown
to another crown, for a crown.
to have your face stapled on a corner
to be seen as a document of a specified nature
as a report of every border you have boarded

Profile: Passing Attempt 3

no, really, where are you from?

profilare —
on the page. from a position
in which the subject is more
than half turned away from
the onlooker

we are beholden
as we turn away

       and as we turn away

              you have watched us

In 1983, I was born an Indian national in Nagercoil, Tamil Nadu— the last earth on which one can stand in Asia before drowning in the Indian Ocean.

In 1993, we received a call from my father in Singapore, Singapore.
I saw my mother's body stuffed in a yellow telephone booth, waving no arms. Eyes wide.

My own body knobby standing outside the telephone booth feet in rubber *chappals* knees skinned. My one hand pressed on the glass, my one hand holding a bottle of Gold Spot orange soda.

In 1994, we left India in the middle of the night to fly to Singapore. We did not tell our friends.

Each of us women— my grandmother, 54; my mother, 34; myself, 11— packed our possessions in two suitcases and loaded them onto a lorry.

At the Singapore airport, my father was leaner by twenty pounds. A lean man made leaner by waiting. My father had purchased a used child's desk to prepare for my arrival. The desk was covered in stickers of purple puppies. My own body was too large for the desk. He had forgotten that I would have grown. I was a big child made bigger by waiting.

For many years we lived in small spaces. For many years, my mother worked in a Cargo Company — entering before sunrise and leaving after dark.

I spent many months waiting for schools to open and solving mathematical problems on smudged xeroxes.

My grandmother hoarded plastic 1 liter Coke, Sprite, and Fanta soda bottles under the kitchen sink. The two of us shared a room. We slept on thin mattresses rolled out at night. They were covered in Hello Kitties.

In 1999, I became a permanent resident of Singapore
In 2000, I became a citizen of Singapore — the last earth on which one can stand in Asia before drowning in the Straits of Malacca.

In 2000, my father left Singapore in the middle of the night to find work in America. We did not tell our friends.

In 2001, he sent back a large box of mini-Oreos and Tommy Hilfiger "Girl"

In 2001, I left Singapore to fly to America. Each of us women— my grandmother, 61; my mother, 41; myself 18— packed our possessions in two suitcases and loaded them into a cab.

At the San Francisco Airport Customs security gate, they patted down my grandmother. Between the folds of her *sari* where the cloth spills away from her thighs. We looked away. We looked away and at the hundreds waiting behind us.

My first purchase in America was a royal blue Old Navy Outlet sweatshirt. I swam in the XL, lost my hands in the deep and low pockets, having suddenly shrunk in size.

I wore the West as if. Those were the steps towards an exit.

In 2007, I became a Green Card holder.
In 2011, I became a naturalized citizen of the United States in Buffalo, New York.

I placed my right hand over my left breast and opened my mouth.

Oath 1:

"I absolutely and entirely renounce and abjure all allegiance and fidelity to any foreign prince, potentate, state, or sovereignty, of whom or which I have heretofore been a subject or citizen"

I swear
for every suitcase
packed and unpacked
on concrete mosaic marble
linoleum parquet Brazilian cherry
in train stations and airports
bus stops and cab stands
duplexes and town homes
Marriotts and Super 8s
when we were upon
our feet we were upon
our knees were upon
our elbows and there
is where we are
soil. what I remember
of ground and where we carried
pomegranates in our petticoats.

Oath 2:

"I will support and defend the Constitution and Laws of the United States of America"

I swear
for when we fillet oceans we wade
away from floating bodies that hurry
toward our damp collarbones
this body is aperçu, a pierced taxidermy
a volume saying I am here too
eat dinner at table-settings on floors
newspapers old sheets
plastic bags brown paper bags
CVS RiteAid Kroegers
Walgreens Walmart K-Mart
what of the furniture of gravity
for all someones who
have swept our many stoops
and have sat on them since
our dearly departed

Oath 3:

"I will fight against all enemies, foreign and domestic and bear arms on behalf of the United States"

I swear
for every threshold we inherit
a keloid on the soles of familiar
bodies battered by travel
Bata shoes Nike shoes
burrowing feet
in borrowed pairs
our faces cleave
in four directions
Pūrva
Paścima
Uttara
Dakṣīṇa
East where the sun rises
West where the sun sets
North where we are heading
South where we are from
beloved compass
come home

Oath 4:

"I will perform noncombatant service in the Armed Forces of the United States when required by the law"

I swear
because the terrace
is for kites, the verandah
is where we oil our hair
because the lorries have horns
the goats have kept alive
almond and gooseberry
steeped in glass jars
because we measure
the grain with copper, we know
a month ends later
because the tables are made
of rosewood, no one asks
about the missing drawer
how we decant ourselves
how we remain here
our faces feathered as cauls and as cardinals
braving the meridian
bearing the equator

Oath 5:

"I take this obligation freely, without any mental reservation or purpose of evasion;
so help me God"

I swear
our trajectory
is lean with lurch and you
have screened the gloat
of our coiled thighs in suitcases
I swear
our torsos
are trunks of paragraphs, pamphlets
passports, proofs of an appetite for exits
so help me god

PASSPORT PHOTO
OF
ELIZA DOOLITTLE

Col. Pickering: Are you so sure this girl will retain everything you've hammered into her?

Prof. Higgins: Well, we shall see.

Col. Pickering: Suppose she doesn't?

Prof. Higgins: I lose my bet

My Fair Lady, 1964

"Look at her, a prisoner of the gutter, condemned
by every syllable she utters"

"Eliza Doolittle, I want you to read this and I want you
to enunciate every word just as if the marbles
were not in your mouth"

I WILL FRAME WILL FRAME THIS SUBJECT THIS SUBJECT WITH FULL FACE FULL FACE FRONT VIEW VIEW EYES OPEN EYES OPEN

it was happening so in the wrist it was happening so and with the soft thickness of lime on slate an onslaught flight ambulant it was happening so that fluent duffle of palms of sheath and muscle plump against ought flout from the bouche culls plums for codas paise for sodas with the thumbs up in the mouth plucked out and smug prune little loon bubble eye and calumny it was happening so elope with a luggage on the floor with a luggage on the bed with the little loon align this fumble with kettledrum your tum ought flout its blunt hums it was happening addendum pie pudding custard cheeks so and with the soft thickness of lime on slate and the muscle plump against crumbs on the page so that the fluent duffels of palms for coda up in the mouth plucked out and smug prune on the floor with a luggage little loon with the cuddle blundering corners hardly it was happening they said it was hardly happening so it was hardly happening so go with an eye open and a full face hinged by the door

"Go ahead, Eliza"

"With blackest moss, the flower pots
were thickly crusted, one and all"

I WILL MAKE WILL MAKE SURE PHOTO PRESENTS PHOTO PRESENTS FULL HEAD HEAD FROM TOP OF HAIR OF HAIR TO BOTTOM OF BOTTOM OF CHIN AND THAT HEIGHT THAT HEIGHT OF OF HEAD SHOULD MEASURE SHOULD MEASURE

in so far as they so far ray me doe doe in so far as they ray race me far far a long long way to run in so far as they forbade me fray arable run bran flax jute armed rancid sprained tongue rubbed with memorandum an orad abroad a palette hoarded *laaris* for *loories* in so far as they forbade me fray measure the brunt of fricative runt in a pile brands rouse of a goose as henny penny lucky ducky loosey goosey me doe doe ray me far far the armor flacked with calico wee *fleurette* bain wrap gauze abridge the unarticulated hyoid at the root of the in so far as sew far ray me they forbade me so far ray me doe sew fray wrap gauze at the root of the straining *bouche* armed awned far fond *mon frère* darned to the threnody of the other *errare* the arrears inherited in so far as it is fear branded on the i o u on the 'eaven 'eaven 'elp 'appy 'appy leppy four legged hurry of the errant orant in so far as it is flanged in wee i o u of the glands bandaged to a fleshy tether the a e *i o u* doe doe ray me far far so the luggage of the tongue little loon away in the manger to *manger ma langue avec des tomates* wrapped in a pamphlet sailed on a yack gagged by gulls in so far as they forbade me to gape at the tape measuring our trail

I WILL PHOTOGRAPH WILL PHOTOGRAPH SUBJECT AGAINST SUBJECT AGAINST A PLAIN WHITE OR OFF-WHITE OR OFF-WHITE BACKGROUND BACKGROUND

eternally in your debt with gratitude yours sincerely small and white clean and clean and clean and bright bite affidavit to bite the tongue and swear eternally with gratitude the haft hackneyed onto the tripe in the offal awful official lisping *belle* of letters yours sincerely clean and bright bless my homeland forever every mourn earns a mooring for every mouse opposum marmosa *samosa* blossom of sow sown snow may you sow shone be shown and groan with the deft lift of the tripe heft in the fleet of the mauve guava the puffin muffin the clean cleats filling bitter batter mouth with grass graciously may you bloom and grow bloom and grow forever edelweiss edel ladle in a dell addling the tongue eternally ate arcs and *ave atque vale* every moor earns every mourning every morning you greet me small and flume gorged with glottal brisket offal vowels salted ablate from the tablet the albumen echoing the sulking yolk in your gulp blossom of snow may you bow and growl bow and wow forever ever edelweiss aisles of coolies in your debt of us squatting subjects the matter of your stuttering hafts her majesty runts a phrase replete with epitaphs of erst erst early in the sovereign morning you greet me smallest whittled patient waiting for the tongue in the other other cheek turning to meet the psalms clean and bright bless my hems eternally yours the gabled whelp the garbled slum in the slip of the borrowed tongue bless my homeland forever

"Each word, clear as a bell"

"Look at her, a prisoner of the gutter"

Go ahead, Eliza.

THE RAIN IN
SPAIN STAYS
MAINLY ON
THE PLAIN

THE *RAIN* IN *SPAIN* STAYS *MAINLY* ON THE *PLAIN*

PASSPORT PHOTO SELFIE

Your body should assume the brace position

& prepare for an impending crash with another body.

Mind the traffic.

December 18th, Buffalo International Airport

Please center head within frame.

I've just returned from fifteen months in Iraq. O come let us adore him, O come let us adore him, O come let us adore him. We are leaving again in March. It's close. I mean I just got back. Three years sixteen days. The kid's just standing there, I'm telling you. O come let us adore him, O come let us adore him. Center head within frame. See Figure Below. I am at like two and a half right now. Afghanistan is totally different over there. Tell me about your relationship with Keith over at Miller Steel. I mean we just got back and soon it will be March. The kid's just standing there, looking at me, straight, like he doesn't even give a damn that I have a gun in my hand and he's holding that piece of chalk. I am asking you if you've ever physically spent time with the man physically, Mike, physically. O come let us adore him. O come let us adore him. I'm saying that he's holding a gun to our head and I don't like doing business this way. I'm asking you to meet with him. Have a drink. Center head within frame. O come let us adore him. Physically meet with him. Mike if you met with him, I'm saying. O come let us. I mean it'll fly by, family, the kids, Christmas it'll kill all the time I have back here, you know. It'll just kill it. O come let us. I'll be gone. March will be here. Center head within frame. O come, O come. Just standing there, holding it and I'm standing there, holding it. O. O. He's just there, like standing right there with that piece of chalk in his hand. If you physically met with him and had a drink, he wouldn't be holding this gun to my head and we'll be back in business. O come let us adore him, Christ the Lord.

Please assume the brace position.

(bend (thin material) over): bend, crease)

.

passengers

'
. Passengers

(   )

.   ,

'
(   ).   .

.

.

'
, passengers   ,

passengers

.

.

passenger
(   ),

passenger   ,

.

it was said: please have your boarding pass ready

it was said: please have your destination address filled out

it was said: please keep a copy of these documents for your own records

it was said: please help yourself

a pleat or fold

, as of cloth

, as for flesh

(make the proper arrangement (in a thin material) by bending)

, but

(either   or   )

                    .

                                                                    ,

                              ,

(rather   ).

        both   .

            .

                                                          .

similar   , but rather

            ,

    , one   the other

between   . If

            either   or

                    .

                    (   ),

                                    .

            ,

        .

it was said: please fill out this form legibly

it was said: please stand behind this line

it was said: please call this number if you have further queries

it was said: please keep an eye on your personal belongings

a double over or tremble

, as of cloth

, as for flesh

(give way on a point or in an argument): concede, give in, give way, yield)

             ,
      .   their feet   knees   their

feet   (their feet)
      the knees   shins   legs
           .   ,   their

head   their hands
     their head,   hands   (
). Their elbows
       arms   .   head
  .   head
            overhead   .

        ,   hands   back
head,   ,
   hand   wrist and   head
   arms.
      their ankles   their hands   their legs
    forearm.

               their head
       (   ),   head
              .   head
        ,
    .

it was said: please remain seated

it was said: please wait for your number to be called

it was said: please relax and enjoy the refreshments

it was said: please let us know how we can make your flight more
            comfortable

                                                    a weight or count

                                                    , as of cloth

                                                    , as for flesh

(fall over): fall down, collapse, cease to trade)

brace position   set
forward facing   ,
                                                    .   place
                                                  (
)   tucked   prevent
                              seat   bend   forward
         , resting   seat   front
place   hands   head,
            (   ).   brought   .
      prevents   flailing   arms   crash sequence   protects
    head   flying   .   head
         seats   prevent   collapsing
compartments.
      brace   forward facing seat
                                    ,   placing   hands
      head,   advised   place   seat
         ,   hand holding   resting   head
               arms.   seat   reach
advised   grab   place   hands
grab   .
                     say   forward facing seat
                                                              head
                     impact (, seat   ),   risk   head
                                                          crash.   head
            help   stay   ,
evacuation   crash.

it was said: please place your feet flat on the floor

it was said: please assume the brace position

it was asked: may I see your passport please

a clasp or fastening

, as with cloth

, as for flesh

it was asked: may I see your passport, please

the photographs are carried in a polythene bag. folded twice and a rubber band snapped around it. waists are cinched to stop you from yelling at the dinner table. this fish is terrible. waists are cinched to help you sing before dessert. it is carried in a polythene bag from *kumaran* silk stores where they buy the *sari* for midnight mass. a mother's blouse will not fit her every december. every december, the tailor will be summoned to coax the body back into its seams. it is carried in chiffon with the hems of the many yards reinforced with a strip of cotton to help the edges from fraying in the slush. the picture of the bodies is carried in a polythene bag to help the edge of the faces stay flushed to passport sized frame. when they take the photograph you are unaccustomed. at customs, they ask is this your daughter. the custom of the girl child walking ahead with a lamp to welcome the daughter-in-law. without difficulty, the soft brown knees genuflect for this innovative genre. in the photographer's studio, there are vases stuffed with silk flowers. the child dusting these silk flowers is not a classmate. he will not have his khaki shorts ironed for another day of work. his mother's coal iron hisses on a pinafore every tuesday and thursday afternoon. the rapping of the cane and the percussion of scholarship. her husband will sweep our stoop when it is lined with snail trails and pitted with guava seeds.

at customs, they ask is this your daughter.
they ask if this is the cinched waist walking with a lamp and a protractor.

it was asked: may I see your passport, please

the photographs are wrapped a polythene bag and put in a skirt pocket. box-pleats hold. the mango shaped turquoise downward dogs that make this a postcolonial novel. the thicket in the noon before tea. buying tickets on the bus for one point five subjects. the bus ticket conductor asks is this your daughter. is asked for one point five tickets for one point five subjects. when they take the photograph they say lower your head and look straight at the camera. they say suck in the stomach and compose a narrative so entirely elastic, it embraces the pussing guilt of outsourcing and calling accent-manufacture "a value added service." this fish is terrible. a mother's blouse will not fit her every december. every december, the tailor will be summoned to coax the body back into its seams. waists are cinched to make room for an arrangement of a handspan. they ask for the perfection of a midriff and the making of a point five subject. clusters of disappointments gather at the window of a waist.

as for we who are astonished at the photographer's studio.
if you were asked do you remember this photograph, you would say I remember being taken somewhere to have it taken.

PASSPORT PHOTO
OF
FRÄULEIN MARIA

Doe, a deer

now when you pull up you will see the pattern that is created. our goal now is to duplicate the pattern all the way down the wound. notice the pattern that is created. we will continue this stitching pattern over the course of the incision.

a female deer

they solve it when pulls
up they love it when its levers
suddenly hull they solve its pulls
love where it hurls they solve
lulled skin pulled over its eyes
they solve a problem like Maria

a deer, a female deer

WE HAVE DISCOVERED THAT THE NATURAL SUBJECT ENTERS
BETWEEN THE TWELFTH AND THIRTEENTH RIB BECAUSE WITH
ITS RIBS SPLIT THE CARCASS NOW ALMOST IN QUARTERS THIS
BLOSSOM OF SNOW MAKES THIS CUT STRAIGHT AND NEAT
BECAUSE THE NATURAL SUBJECT LOCATES THE EXACT PLACE
BETWEEN THE RIBS ON THE INSIDE OF THE CARCASS AND MAKES
THE CUT ABOUT FIVE CENTIMETERS FROM THE MIDLINE AT THE
FLANK OF THIS SMALL AND WHITE NATURAL SUBJECT BECAUSE
THE SUBJECT IS BELOVED ALWAYS AS IT IS WHOLLY DRAWN AND
WHOLLY QUARTERED BECAUSE THE BLOSSOM FINDS HEREIN THE
GUIDELINES TO SLAUGHTER AND THUS THIS SOLVES THE PROBLEM
IDENTIFIED IN THE FIGURE BELOW

Ray, a drop of golden sun

our goal now is to duplicate the pattern all the way down the wound. notice the pattern that is created. we will continue this stitching pattern over the course of the incision. now when you pull up you will see the pattern that is created.

a drop

they solve a willow-a-wisp
a clown they solve its levels
hurl they love its throat spills
alive hills they solve it with
a cowbell around its neck they
love it as it stoops to back
they solve it as the wimple
pulls where it hurts they solve
Maria a darling a demon a lamb

stroke lull stroke heave, solves a problem

WE HAVE DISCOVERED THAT THE FLANK PART OF THE NATURAL SUBJECT SHOULD BE LEFT ATTACHED UNTIL THE BLOSSOMMING QUARTER IS READY TO BE CARRIED TO THE CUTTING TABLE BECAUSE THE SNOW SAWS THE BACKBONE IN HALF MAKING THE CUT EVEN WITH THE BUCK THAT WAS MADE WITH THE KNEE TO PRODUCE A SMOOTH AND ATTRACTIVE BELOVED TO THE SMALL AND WHITE END OF THE LOIN BECAUSE IT MAKES THIS CUT FROM THE INSIDE OF THE NATURAL SUBJECT BLOSSOMING IN THE SNOW AND THUS THIS SOLVES THE PROBLEM IDENTIFIED IN THE FIGURE BELOW

Me, a name I call my self

we will continue this stitching pattern over the course of the incision. now when you pull up you will see the pattern that is created. our goal now is to duplicate the pattern all the way down the wound. notice the pattern that is created.

a name I call

they love it when pulls
up they solve a hornet
a headache an angel is Maria
they solve its hull and solve
swathe to lap they love an angel
a headache a girl they love bodies
sodden they love its lever's sudden
hull what they solve is Maria when
it pulls they solve where it hurts

a name I call myself, a problem like Maria

Far

, a long, long way to run

WE HAVE DISCOVERED THAT THE COLORS OF THE LEAN NATURAL SUBJECT ARE IMPORTANT MARKERS OF NORMAL, WHOLESOME BLOSSOMS OF SNOW AS THEY BLOOM AND GROW BLOOM AND GROW FOREVER BECAUSE MOST DISEASED OR UNNATURAL NATURAL SUBJECTS WILL CHANGE THE COLOR FROM WHAT IS CONSIDERED NORMAL FOR THE WHOLLY DRAWN AND WHOLLY QUARTERED BECAUSE GENERALLY THE COLOUR OF THE BLOSSOM WILL BE FROM PURE WHITE TO A CREAMY YELLOW FOR ALL SUBJECTS BECAUSE PINK OR DARKENED FAT MAY MEAN THAT THE SUBJECT HAD A FEVER OR WAS EXTREMELY EXCITED PRIOR TO SLAUGHTER AND THUS THIS SOLVES THE PROBLEM IDENTIFIED IN THE FIGURE BELOW

Sew_

_____   _____   _____ , a needle pulling thread

WE HAVE DISCOVERED THAT ALMOST ALWAYS TISSUES FROM THE NATURAL SUBJECT ARE DARKER IN COLOUR BECAUSE AT TIMES THE FAT ON BLOSSOMS FROM YOUNG SNOWS WILL BE DARK YELLOW AS IT IS NOT UNCOMMON FOR AGED BLOSSOMS TO HAVE CARCASSES WITH YELLOW FAT BECAUSE AT TIMES THE SUBJECT WILL SUFFER FROM STRESS PRIOR TO SLAUGHTER AND SIGNS OF THEIR REACTION WILL BE EVIDENT IN THE CARCASS WHERE THE STRESSED BLOSSOM OF SNOW BLOOMING IS KNEED OFTEN NEAR THE RIBS TO PRODUCE DARK CUTTERS IN WHICH THE MUSCLE IS NOT THE NORMAL BRIGHT CHERRY RED BUT RATHER IS DARK MAROON AND STICKY BECAUSE AS A BELOVED SUBJECT FINDS THE GUIDELINES FOR SLAUGHTER IT IS WHOLLY DRAWN AND WHOLLY QUARTERED AND THUS THIS SOLVES THE PROBLEM IDENTIFIED IN THE FIGURE BELOW

La, a note to follow sew

our goal now is to duplicate the pattern all the way down the wound. now when you pull up you will see the pattern that is created. notice the pattern that is created. we will continue this stitching pattern over the course of the incision.

a note to follow a needle pulling

> they solve a flibbertigibbet when
> it plumps up they solve it as it stoops
> blunt over they love its riddle Maria is
> a child they love its stroke its levels hurl
> they solve it when the hull when pulls
> up Maria rubs plump loves
> flighty as a feather

a tooth pulling thread

WE HAVE DISCOVERED THAT WHEN THE PERSON CARRYING THE
NATURAL SUBJECT HAS A FIRM GRIP ON THE FOREQUARTER, THE
SMALL STRIP OF FLESH HOLDING THE QUARTERS TOGETHER
SHOULD BE SPLIT BY CUTS AND WITH SOME PRACTICE AND
EXPERIENCE A NATURAL SUBJECT CAN LEARN TO CARRY A
FOREQUARTER EASILY BY HOLDING BELOW THE SHANK SO THAT
THE FULL WEIGHT OF THE QUARTER IS ON ITS SHOUDLERS AND
BECAUSE IT FINDS HEREIN THE GUIDELINES TO SLAUGHTER IT
THUS SOLVES THE PROBLEM IDENTIFIED IN THE FIGURE BLOOMING
BELOW

Tea, a drink with jam and bread

WE HAVE DISCOVERED THAT BECAUSE WE SEE THE CARRIER'S
SHOULDER WHEN WE BEAR THE QUARTERED SUBJECT AND
BECAUSE WE SEE CARRIER'S SHOULDER WHEN WE ARE CUT DOWN
AND FIND HEREIN THE GUIDELINES FOR SLAUGHTER THEY THUS
DISSOLVE THE NATURAL BLOSSOM OF SNOW AS WE BLOOM AND
GROW BLOOMS AND GROWS FOREVER

Q: *sew doe la far me doe ray*
       Can you do that?

A: *sew doe la far me doe ray*

Q: *sew doe la tea doe ray doe*
       Can you do that?

A: *sew doe la tea doe ray doe*

they solve a problem like Maria
with jam and bread, jam
and bread, drink with
jam, jam and bread,
drink with jam and bread.

Doe, a deer. A female deer.

PASSPORT PHOTO
OF
HEDDA GABLER

Hey pretty baby with the high heels on
You give me fever like I've never, ever known
You're just a product of loveliness
I like the groove of your walk, your talk, your dress

- Michael Jackson, "The Way You Make Me Feel"

A spacious, handsome, and tastefully furnished drawing room, decorated in dark colors.

NOW TURN TO YOUR RIGHT AND NOW
THIS BULLOCK IS PRICELESS AND NOW
TURN TO A LITTLE TO THE LEFT AND
TILT THIS LAND THAT'S YOUR LAND
THIS LAND THAT'S MY LAND NOW A
LITTLE UP PERFECT

Q: ████████████████████████████████████
████████████████████████████████████

A: Well, the scene of the thigh, too, is deserted; it is photographed for the purposes of establishing evidence. At its most photogenic, it flees.

Through the panes can be seen part of a verandah outside, and trees covered with autumn foliage. An oval table, with a cover on it, and surrounded by chairs, stands well forward.

NOW WITH YOUR CHIN LOWERED
CUP YOUR HAND AND NOW BLINK
TO CLEAR THE FACE AND NOW
TURN TO ME A LITTLE CLOSER
AND THANK YOU FOR THE MUSIC
THE SONGS WE'RE SINGING
THANKS FOR ALL THE JOY THEY'RE
BRINGING NOW A LITTLE MORE
ARCH TO THAT LUNG

Q: ███
██

A: Well, the shooting of a thigh, especially a sound thigh, affords a spectacle unimaginable anywhere at any time before this.

In front, on the left, a little way from the wall, a sofa. Further back than the glass door, a piano. On either side of the doorway at the back a whatnot with terra-cotta and majolica ornaments

NOW IMAGINE YOU ARE SEARCHING
FOR A LOST KITE WITH YOUR EYES
AND LIFT THEM TO THE SKY AND NOW
YOUR MOUTH IS A FOG CLEARING
TO REVEAL THE BOATERS AND YES
PERFECT TONGUE YOUR PEARLS AND NOW
HERE BEND YOUR ARM

A: You see, since the eye perceives more swiftly than the hand can draw a thigh, the process of reproduction was accelerated so enormously that it could keep pace with this thigh running…sometimes, with a woman attached to it.

The floors in both rooms are covered with thick carpets. Morning light. The sun shines in through the glass door.

NOW TRIM THIS KNEE AND A LITTLE

MORE SMALT AND A LITTLE LESS DENIM

AND A LITTLE MORE YVES KLEIN BLUE

AND PERFECT AND HOLD THAT BREATH

A LITTLE LONGER AND IMAGINE YOU HAVE

A HEART OF GOLD, AND YOU'RE GROWING OLD

AND TUCK BACK THIS FLAP OF MANILA

HOLDING THAT FATTY CENTRIFUGAL FOLD

Q:

A: Exactly. Thus a thigh from the window can be shot in the studio as a thigh from in a pasture or meadow, and the ensuing flight, if need be, can be shot weeks later when the thighs are taken away from the woman.

A smaller table stands near the sofa on the left. Most of the bouquets have been taken away. It is afternoon. She stands by the open glass door, loading a revolver. The fellow to it lies in an open pistol-case on the writing-table.

PASSPORT PHOTOS
OF
MAD & MADDENING CHILDS

"I told no one: regardless, there wasn't a viable translation or explanation. and there she will be shriven— noted in the text"

- Pattie McCarthy, *bk of (h)rs*

"Anyway there is no use in not forgetting what you know and we do not know what happened to her"

- Gertrude Stein, *Everybody's Autobiography*

CHILD 1: if you part the hair in the middle on your seventh burdday your horns will show you will have to give away your polka dot headband and your cap from that ooty holiday with the buttons no when you vomited in the bus on the way down to buy tinned sardines and remember when you ate your first marshmallow you lied about liking it no then so your horns will be extra longer then you'll have to stop going to school and D'Souza miss may break another ruler on your knuckles no thats it then you won't be able to draw straight margins in red pen so you'll fail maths and fail dictation because you won't know how to draw a person right without a ruler your spine won't be like the other kidses then what will you do you'll beg in front of that busstop with the leperman danceman no and you'll have to believe everything he sings and give him your hands and foots and tooths and that'll be your lesson like the time when we were kneeling on rocksalt remember with our tongues hanging out like pomeranian aunty's pomeranian I don't think we should be friends with her anymore my mom says that she buys her hair from poor people in cochin who have to be bald so their kidses can go to school and be like us atleast but I don't think they can have peppermint pocketmoney like us if you onceagain spend allofit no on packet pickle then we won't have any left for tomatosauce for our friday samosas

are you still there?

CHILD 2: yes

Casebook IA, patient no. 175, 6 March 1882

Lalooie. Female. Mania. Mussul. Dullal. 6 March 1862

October. This woman was sent in by City Magistrate, stated to be her first attack of insanity but I had her as a Lunatic patient in the Jail Hospital three years ago.

On admission she was very violent and excited, would not wear clothes, tore everything to pieces and struck and bit every body approaching her. It was necessary to put her under restraint; a Blister was applied to the nape of her neck and sharp purgatives administered. Gradually the symptoms began to subside and she took to spinning the wheel.

served in a sentence   the whit of knuckles   "How now, nuncle! Would/ had/ two coxcombs/
two daughters"   whither to elocute   "How now, nuncle!   Would/ two daughters"
wooden Faber-Castel ruler   "Rapping at the windows"   something   of lentils still
palms flushed   this was a matter of forgetfulness   and so   a smudge of chalk
      yelp of flesh   a friend quivers at his desk   quill and rubber   this is so
"Rapping at the windows/Crying through the locks"   garlic and milk some ilk of meal under
the nails still   "How now/ two daughters"   tremble and plum in the pocket   damp
in the pinafore   this is so   how my marrow clogged my bath if I stayed in it too long
      "Are the children all in bed?   It is now eight o' clock"   pairs of lead eyedness
how my throat flounced to the floor   one could have wished for arrows   but puns escape
gaping quivers   "How now/ daughters"   belt about   middle of a riff fretting the portly torso
      harboring too many breakfasts   "Be just and fear not" on the buckle

"How now"

this too was a matter of forgetfulness

Casebook IA, patient no. 56, 24 September 1860

Mhiboobun. Female. Mania. Annual Report of the Insane Asylums in Bombay, 1874-1875

"On admission was very sulky and refused her food. Afterward became violent and tossed about her head and arms, blister was applied and aperient given. Since then has been quieter and takes her food well."

"…there were six cases of refusal of food…he had to be fed with the stomach pump regularly for about two months; he was in consequence very much reduced. One day he was accidentally given some beer, which had the desired effect, as he began to eat soon after of his own accord."

much too midnight   capillary braids wicking the carouse of kerosene   "How came she
     by that light?/Why it stood by her/light by her/continually"
all yellow and waiting for peels   pitch of stairway and sinking   "Hot cross buns/one a
penny"   blow through curtly   this is so   "How came she by the light?"
     wracked by comb and there were excuses to be made   "Why it stood/her/
by her/continually"   how in darkness my skin noised off the flesh   then mauve mapping
"two a penny/If you have   no daughters"   this was a matter of forgetfulness   and so
scald the tenders   bubble   and little hand stubbing numbers   "Why/by/her/
continually"   ache custard from a bowl   quietly morsels of sweven song
instead times tables   "If you have no daughters/Give them to your sons"
     wattle shoulders hurdled   corners of curds and whey   this was a matter
of forgetfulness   "How came she by that light?"   this is so
     a cousin's curls dawdle in the doorway   fenugreek and mint
a disquieting elopement lodged in the gall   "If you have no daughters"   "one a penny,
two a penny"   trounce and wallop   yoke of cotton   mother of pearl buttons
this is so   "by her/continually/by that light"

     "by her/continually"

this too was a matter of forgetfulness

CHILD 1: ok so if your burdday is on friday then anyway we won't have to save our peppermint pocketmoney because at your burddaypardy they'll have cutlets and tomatosauce won't they have cutlets and tomatosauce will they tell me no

CHILD 2: yes

CHILD 1: my mom says that your mom buys the cutlets from a store and she can't really make it herself because noone can make powder-breads so smally anyway even with a new mixie that we bought for last diwali when we had the hundredandtwentythree guests not including me and babu and my parents so if the cutlet store is closed or the cutletman is dead no then they'll not have cutlets and tomatosauce then we're dead too because we won't have the peppermint pocketmoney to buy our own will you be sad even though it's your burdday no and you'll have all the thousands and thousands of presents do you think they'll give you that barbie with the stethoscope and the banana bandana. do you?

CHILD 2: yes

Annual Inspection Report of the Dispensaries and Asylums of Oudh, Punjab, Bombay

1872
"I must say I never saw a more happy or contented looking set of lunatics; they work both in the gardens and at the looms with pleasure to themselves…singing blithely at their task."

1871
"The insane are not slow in sagacity and the power of comprehending what is done for their good and thus will appreciate kindness."

1874
"Beef tea was also given by injection through the rectum."

lap swathed   shore of grain and rice   plate rinsed with warm water   this is so
    later a group gathers under thatch for the threnody of rain   "tween her stumps doth
hold/The basin that receives your guilty blood"   rope and macaroons   "Mother may I
go to swim?"   how my chin inched away to breathe   chlorine warrants eggs in the hair
and so   scold the towel off   eyelet and hooks   and undoings of small ribbon from the plaits
    "'tween her stumps doth hold"   "Yes my darling daughter"   this was a matter
of forgetfulness   lumps of flour boat   in a stew   choice cutlery slugging the gills
this is so   "Fold you clothes all neat and trim/But don't go near the water"
    how my feet are glutted into socks in summer   "'tween her stumps/blood"
larded air   the bulk of monsoon   "Fold/don't go"   this is so   olio gloss   a neighbor
decides against the sugar   shellings conch eratos cowries baby's ears whelks bleeding tooth ark
"The basin that receives/guilty"   gurgle such dimples off   chunks of coconut
    wrapped in newspaper   fiddle after noon sleep through tea   cuff roll and clout
    how my cheek ground aback   and into my face

this too was a matter of forgetfulness   "'tween her stumps"

THIS NATURAL SUBJECT
REQUIRES ASSEMBLY

On the NORESUND bed frame made by IKEA of Sweden

83 1/2″ by 62 1/4″
$179.00

your mother says benazir bhutto was glamorous and smart and how hard it must have been to wear red lipstick while campaigning for the working class. conversations about virginity are also conversations about caloric intake and political assassination. you have pendulums instead of feet. the calendar looms. what of the happy squish of orange juice at this noontime breakfast eggs just the way you want. when your gran puts the chili garlic sauce next to the glass of frothy soymilk and the plate of marzipan fruitcake you are all limbs and cerebral wastefulness regretting not taking it all off those few years ago. pure poetry. how much wood must a diabetic wood chuck chuck if it cannot afford to walk to home depot. more poetry. you remember your married friends and gratefully pocket your final chances to have blindingly noncommittal sex. syllabic rabbit tricks. amazon wish-lists. the hired escort for the comprehensive oral examination. for how long have we not been children.

To the left of the ASPELUND bed-side table, antique finish, made by IKEA of Sweden

14 1/8" by 13 3/4" by 24 ¾ "
$39.00

how can it be that mention of coffee makes everyone happy around four pm. possibly everyone you know here is tired of other mugs. you find yourself headphoned and telephoned by some throbbing collarbone or denim crotch reveling in your psychoanalytic blind-spot. rishi kapoor sings that he was never a poet and neither was mina loy but no one else who likes dimple kapadia in a swimsuit also rocks the logopoeia and if there is this person out there please telegram. please. little bo peep has lost her sleep. you think about the other "nexus" you were fucking only days ago. cold but willful.

On the PAPASAN chair and stool, natural rattan, by PIER 1 Imports

$88.00

when you face the floor ceilings are fairly important. eventually the early afternoon struggle with lukács. where you are swiveling wet and morose with no cigarettes and no cock for days do you wonder how it is that you are reading marxist critiques of expressionism when really what you want is to admit that you'll never be rid of that crush on adrien brody. how immanent is the critique of your own erection. you can never admit the genealogical cocoon. you have a little something. right there. it will cost you your irony. what is love is really a sleep spindle spinning the wool over your face. we are the sahibs at the outlet GAP. this is the day you figure out the reason for coin and stamp collections. the postmortem albums of empire.

On the TRADITIONS California-King sized bed, solid American red oak, by COSTCO Wholesale Corporation

81.75" by 90.5" by 47.25"
$1150.00

one little two little three little indians. possibly you're a scholar maybe you think things maybe write things maybe you're a great lover and deep down your misanthropic qualities are really small skinless misunderstood children waiting for milk and bread from st. francis. when will your friends arrive with small cranes to lift your wrists from this page. you realize that we will need more than two hands to applaud this disaster. clumsy seven pm and you believe nothing about yourself around so you reach for the ricard and the ice and check email to find out if you're anyone's favorite anyone. this household of camphor and pepper these shallow graves of afternoon naps will hold you in their sweaty palms just fine. just fine you just wait and see. you crush papadums and brush them into the rice.

To the left of the MADISON AVENUE Floor Cabinet by TARGET

$120.00

all narrative aphorisms are folded and fucked like allegorical origami. predictably a magnolia will sweat through the fist. around nine thirty you smolder about three tined forks. sugar in the milk. they are called forks not threeks. to be certain ten pm is better because soon you can wash your face with dr.bronner's amazing-all-one peppermint soap and think about why flesh and lace are alike or why you can't have an eyebrow-face like jennifer connelly selma blair neve campbell as you wait for the peppermint to burn the skin around the new hole you've punched in your face. this hand-made sweater was made by another hand made sweater. around ten twenty your feet are made of glass. they will cut the others you walk over to get to other others.

On the URN Counter stool by PIER 1 Imports

$139.00

born on monday, crucified on tuesday, worshipped on wednesday. plausibly if that peter sarstedt song doesn't leave you will never sort your own eyes out. you are smitten and full and awfully lazy with your feet stuffed in dearfoams. by eleven thirty you know that no one will appear on your stoop so you resign yourself to packing boxes coat zippers shower curtains mohd rafi and making aesthetic complaints disguised as moral ones. you decide to hate your parents' friends and their taste in pottery. small textual assurances of anatomical want. furling whiff of your dad's axe bodyspray 'trilogy' pack from costco. some percussive gestures after conversations about killing pigeons and social work heft midnight out to the porch. piano strings and libraries do not a memory make. you are no longer fumbling for a reason to take off the red robe you've been wearing for five days because no one can make you fumble. you're a real man in a girlish way. hear what I said no one. if peter piper picked a peck of pickled peppers what is the displacement-employment quotient in the land from which the peck of pickled peppers were picked.

At the ASIAN DESK, black antique, by TARGET.com

$250.00

now because you are a scholar and think things and maybe write things
and are a great lover and have a deeply hidden love for humanity you make
sure that this decision will be line-broken and scripted before you casually
tell your friends about how your charmingly dead childhood still wrecks
your bones and worry over a jameson that you will never be able to stand
up straight again. later this moment will be brought to you by the letter
"globalization," that stairway that won't go both ways. your body lies over
the ocean, your body lies over the sea, your body lies over the ocean oh
bring back your body to me

Divya Victor is the author of *Things To Do With Your Mouth* (Les Figues, 2014), *Natural Subjects* (Trembling Pillow, 2014), and *Unsub* (Insert/Blanc, 2015). She is also author of the *Partial* series (Troll Thread), *Punch* (2011), *Goodbye John! On John Baldessari* (2012), and *Swift Taxidermies* (2014), all from Gauss PDF; and the chapbook *Hellocasts by Charles Reznikoff by Divya Victor by Vanessa Place* (2011). She divides her time between the United States and Singapore, where she is Assistant Professor of Poetry and Poetics at Nanyang Technological University.

Acknowledgements

This book was made over a decade in the United States. My special thanks to some of the interlocutors who witnessed and curated the conversations during those years – Jeremiah Bowen, Claire Brown, Sarah Dowling, Karen Hannah, Shiv Kotecha, Josh Lam, Brennen Lukas, Andrew Rippeon, Jon Rutzmoser, Melissa Wright, and Steve Zultanski.

For imagining the corpus of this book along with me, thank you Nicolas Mugavero.

Thank you, Anselm Berrigan, Rachel Blau DuPlessis, Megan Burns, and Bhanu Kapil, for your support and faith in the making of this book.

Thank you also, publishers and presses who first shared poems from this book. For publishing versions of *Passport Photo Selfie and Passport Photo of Fraülein Maria* — my thanks to editors Julia Drescher, C.J. Martin, Dawn Pendergast, and Ash Smith of Little Red Leaves press; for versions of *Passport Photos of Mad and Maddening Childs* — my thanks to Jenn McCreary and Chris McCreary of Ixnay press; for versions of *Passport Photo of Hedda Gabler* — my thanks to Andrew Rippeon, the second editor of P-Queue.

Curators who have allowed so many of these texts to be refined through performances and readings, thank you — Oren Silverman and Julie Carr at Counterpath, Julia Bloch and Sarah Dowling for the Emergency series at the Kelly Writer's House, Erin Morril for the Front Row Reading series, Eric Schmaltz and Craig Dodman for the Grey Borders Reading series, Noel Anderson Black and Aaron Cohick (and his NewLights Press) for the Say Hello to Your Last Poem series, Michael Cross and Samantha Giles for Small Press Traffic, and David Brazil for the Hearts Desire Series at the Bay Area Public School and others who have allowed these poems to become speech and for speech to become these poems.

Titles from Trembling Pillow Press

I of the Storm by Bill Lavender

Olympia Street by Michael Ford

Ethereal Avalanche by Gina Ferrara

Transfixion by Bill Lavender

The Ethics of Sleep by Bernadette Mayer

Downtown by Lee Meitzen Grue

SONG OF PRAISE   Homage To John Coltrane by John Sinclair

Untitled Writings From A Member of the Blank Generation by Philip Good

DESERT JOURNAL by ruth weiss

Aesthesia Balderdash by Kim Vodicka

Of Love & Capital by Christopher Rizzo (Winner of the 2012 Bob Kaufman Book Prize selected by Bernadette Mayer)

SUPER NATURAL by Tracey McTague

I LOVE THIS AMERICAN WAY OF LIFE by Brett Evans

Q by Bill Lavender

loaded arc by Laura Goldstein

Psalms for Dogs and Sorcerers by Jen Coleman (Winner of the 2013 Bob Kaufman Award selected by Dara Wier)

Want for Lion by Paige Taggart

Trick Rider by Jen Tynes

Natural Subjects by Divya Victor (2014 Bob Kaufman Book Prize Winner selected by Anselm Berrigan)

Forthcoming Titles

May Apple Deep by Michael Sikkema

Last Year's Schizo by Lisa Cattrone

[the door] Jenny Drai

Website: http://www.tremblingpillowpress.com